The subject matt
vocabulary have
with expert assis
brief and simple text is printed
in large, clear type.

Children's questions are
anticipated and facts presented
in a logical sequence. Where
possible, the books show
what happened in the past
and what is relevant today.

Special artwork has been
commissioned to set a standard
rarely seen in books for this
reading age and at this price.

Full-colour illustrations are on
48 pages to give maximum
impact and provide the
extra enrichment that is the
aim of all Ladybird Leaders.

A Ladybird Leader
water

Written by James Webster
Illustrated by Gerald Witcomb

Publishers: Ladybird Books Ltd . Loughborough
© Ladybird Books Ltd 1973
Printed in England

More than half the world is covered by water

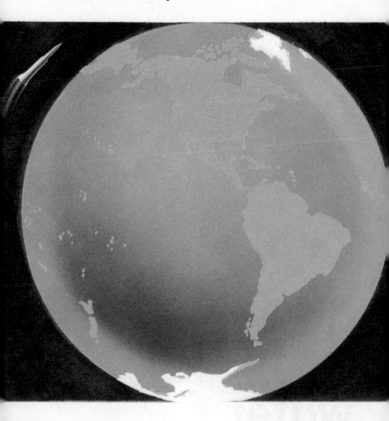

A spaceman might see the world like this.

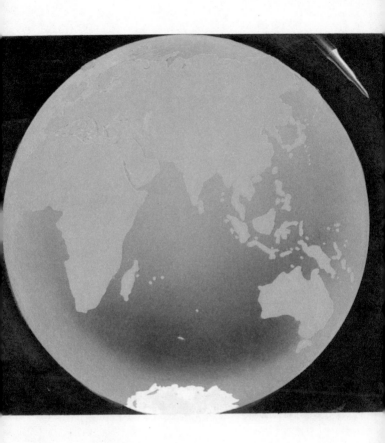

He might see it like this.
He sees that there is much more
water than land.

Where rain comes from

Air over the sea is damp.

The sun warms the damp air
which then rises and cools.

Clouds are then formed.

Clouds are made of tiny water droplets.
When the droplets get bigger,
they fall as rain.

Every living thing needs water

We cannot live without water.
People, animals, birds and insects
must have water.

Elephants wash and cool themselves
with water.

There is water in every living thing

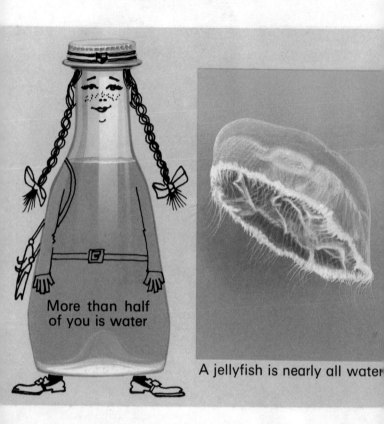

More than half
of you is water

A jellyfish is nearly all water

Most of your body is flesh and blood.
Most fruit and vegetables are
pulp and juice.
Flesh and blood, pulp and juice
are mostly water.

How plants and trees get water

Rain soaks into the soil.
Trees draw it up through their roots.
Flowers draw it through their roots
or stems.
Leaves can take in water.

Plants die without water

without water

with water

a cactus

Deserts are very dry.

Only plants like the cactus can live in deserts.

A cactus can store water.

How people got water long ago

a stream

a man with buckets

a pump

a well

In olden days, people had to live near a stream or river.

Later some had a pump or a well.

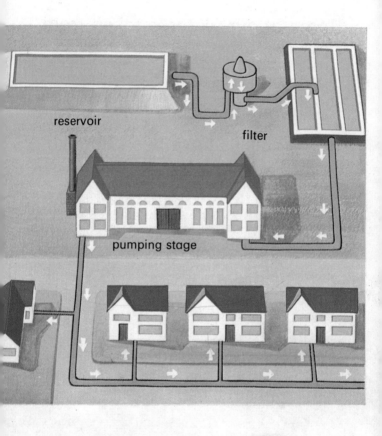

reservoir

filter

pumping stage

Today, water comes to us in pipes.
We just turn a tap to get water.

Where our water comes from

Some of our water is taken from rivers.

Some comes from reservoirs.

Reservoirs are lakes made by man.

Some valleys have been flooded to make reservoirs.

Water that you drink

All drinks have water in them.
Milk is nearly all water.
So are tea and coffee.
Think of some other drinks.

Water that you cannot drink

Shipwrecked sailors must not drink
sea-water.

It is too salt.

They can have water all round them
and still die of thirst.

Water in the kitchen

Meals would be very different withou water.

There would be no boiled eggs,
no boiled vegetables and no jellies.

a washing machine

a dishwasher

another sort of dishwasher!

Clothes and dishes could not
be washed without water.

Water for washing

You need water
to have a bath,
to clean your teeth,
or wash your hair.

Water for warmth

a radiator

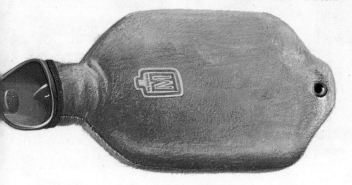

a hot water bottle

Water can keep you warm.
Hot water radiators and
hot water bottles give out heat.

Water for cleaning

Water cleans easily.

We wash many things with it.

Think of some things we wash
with water.

Water in factories

It takes about 15,000 litres of water
to make a set of heavy tyres.

It takes 10,000 litres of water
to make a car *(without tyres)*.

Factories use millions of litres
of water.

More water will have to be found.

Pure water is getting scarce.

Water always flows down

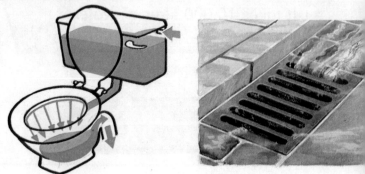

Rivers flow down to the sea.
Water from toilets and drains
flows down to sewers.

See what happens

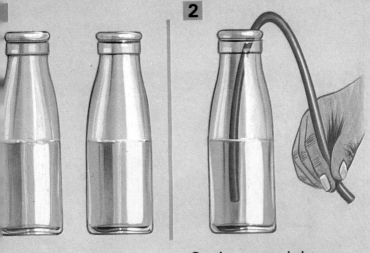

Half fill two bottles

2

Suck water right up a tube. Pinch the end.

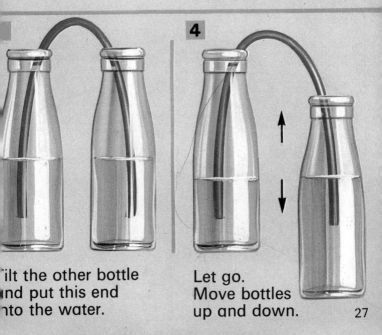

Tilt the other bottle and put this end into the water.

4

Let go.
Move bottles up and down.

Power from water

Falling water can turn turbine engines
to make electricity.

a power station worked by water

Water can turn to steam

When water is heated it turns to steam.

You can see this when a kettle boils.

Power from steam

Some ships are driven by
steam turbines.

Some trains are still pulled by
steam engines.

Water can freeze

a hailstone

an ice crystal

a snowflake

an iceberg

Water takes up more space when it freezes.

This can crack a pipe.

When the ice melts, the pipe leaks.

Ice can be thick enough to skate on.

Water can be dangerous

boiling water is dangerous

fog is water droplets

thin ice can break

Boiling water is dangerous.

Fog, ice and snow on the roads are dangerous.

Thin ice is dangerous.

Heavy rainstorms and high tides
may cause flooding.
Homes and roads can be
washed away.

Saving life from water

a life-jacket

a lifeboat

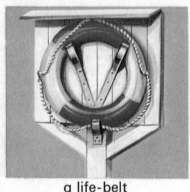

a life-belt

a helicopter

Here are some of the ways that life is saved from water.

At dangerous places there are often life-belts or a life-line.

Saving life with water

People can be trapped in burning buildings.
Firemen try to put out the flames with powerful water-jets.

Water for cooling

An ice-lollipop can cool your mouth.
Cold water can cool your body.
Water cools some car engines.

Water, steam and cooling

In these towers, steam from the power station is cooled.

It becomes water and can be used again.

Water for pleasure

Life would be dull without water.

We would have no fishing, boating, swimming or winter sports.

Snow is frozen water.

Water can be a home

fish have gills

the seal has lungs

Many things make their homes in water.

Some can stay under the water all the time.

Others come up for air.